# contents

**NZ, Canada, US and UK readers**
Please note that Australian cup and
spoon measurements are metric.
A conversion chart appears on page 62.

# rösti with smoked salmon

800g sebago potatoes, peeled
15g butter, melted
1 tablespoon finely chopped fresh dill
½ cup (125ml) olive oil
¾ cup (200g) crème fraîche
200g smoked salmon, sliced
dill for garnish, extra

1  Coarsely grate potatoes, squeeze out excess liquid. Combine potato, butter and dill in medium bowl.
2  Heat a little of the oil in large frying pan. Place an oiled 6cm-round metal cutter in pan and fill with 1 tablespoon of potato mixture, pressing with back of spoon to flatten. Remove cutter carefully (it will be hot) and repeat with remaining oil and potato mixture. Cook rösti until golden on each side; drain on absorbent paper.
3  To serve, place one teaspoon of crème fraîche on each rösti; top with salmon and extra dill.

**preparation time** 30 minutes
**cooking time** 25 minutes
**makes** 24
**per rösti**  7.1g fat; 387kJ (92 cal)
**tip**  Recipe is best made close to serving.

# fish fingers with potato and pea mash

1kg ling fillets, skinned,
    chopped coarsely
2 tablespoons coarsely
    chopped fresh chives
1 teaspoon curry powder
½ cup (75g) plain flour
2 eggs, beaten lightly
2 tablespoons milk
⅔ cup (70g) packaged
    breadcrumbs
⅔ cup (60g) desiccated coconut
vegetable oil, for shallow-frying
potato and pea mash
1kg potatoes, chopped coarsely
1 cup (125g) frozen peas
40g butter
½ cup (125ml) milk

1  Grease 19cm x 29cm slice pan.
2  Process fish, chives and curry powder, pulsing, until mixture forms a smooth paste. Using spatula, press mixture evenly into pan; turn onto baking-paper-lined tray. Cut into eight 19cm slices; cut each slice in half to make 16 fingers.
3  Pat fish fingers with flour, shaking away excess carefully; dip into combined egg and milk then in combined breadcrumbs and coconut.
4  Heat oil in large frying pan; shallow-fry fish fingers, in batches, until browned lightly and cooked through. Drain on absorbent paper.
5  Meanwhile, make potato and pea mash. Serve with fish fingers.
**potato and pea mash**  Boil, steam or microwave potato and peas, separately, until tender; drain. Mash potato in large bowl with butter and milk until smooth. Mash peas in small bowl until crushed. Add peas to potato mash; using wooden spoon, gently stir peas through potato.

**preparation time** 35 minutes
**cooking time** 20 minutes
**serves** 4
**per serving**  61.5g fat; 4400kJ (1051 cal)

# macadamia prawn cakes

¾ cup (180ml)
   orange juice
¼ cup (60ml) lemon juice
2cm piece fresh ginger
   (10g), chopped coarsely
1 teaspoon black
   peppercorns
2 tablespoons white
   vinegar
½ cup (125ml)
   dry white wine
½ cup (75g) roasted
   macadamias
750g cooked peeled
   small prawns
1 egg, beaten lightly
1 tablespoon finely
   grated orange rind
4 green onions,
   chopped finely
1½ cups (110g) stale
   breadcrumbs
1 long loaf pide
2 tablespoons
   vegetable oil
4 egg yolks
250g butter, melted
80g watercress

1  Combine juices, ginger, peppercorns, vinegar and wine in small saucepan; bring to a boil. Reduce heat; simmer, uncovered, about 8 minutes or until mixture reduces to ½ cup. Remove from heat; strain into small jug.

2  Meanwhile, blend or process nuts until finely chopped; place in large bowl. Blend or process 500g of the prawns until mixture forms a paste; place in bowl with nuts. Add remaining prawns, egg, rind, onion and 1 cup of the breadcrumbs; using hands, shape mixture into eight cakes. Press remaining breadcrumbs onto both sides of cakes; place on tray.

3  Cut bread into four pieces; split each piece in half horizontally. Toast, cut-side up, under hot grill until browned lightly; cover to keep warm.

4  Heat oil in large frying pan; cook cakes, in batches, until browned both sides and heated through. Cover to keep warm.

5  Meanwhile, blend or process egg yolks with citrus reduction until combined. With motor operating, add butter in thin, steady stream; process until sauce thickens.

6  Place two pieces of toast on each serving plate; top with watercress then two cakes and drizzle with sauce.

**preparation time** 30 minutes
**cooking time** 30 minutes
**serves** 4
**per serving** 80.9g fat; 4943kJ (1181 cal)

# south-east asian salmon parcels

½ small leek (100g)
⅓ cup loosely packed fresh
  coriander leaves
1 large red capsicum (350g),
  sliced thinly
1 teaspoon five-spice powder
½ teaspoon ground coriander
1 tablespoon grated
  palm sugar
1 tablespoon lime juice
4 x 220g salmon fillets,
  skin removed
4 x 21.5cm-square
  spring roll wrappers
1 tablespoon cornflour
2 teaspoons water
⅓ cup (80ml) peanut oil
2 medium mangoes (860g),
  chopped coarsely
100g red coral lettuce

1  Cut leek into 8cm lengths; halve each piece lengthways then slice halves into thin strips. Combine leek in small bowl with fresh coriander and half the capsicum.

2  Preheat oven to 200°C/180°C fan-forced.

3  Heat small lightly oiled frying pan; cook five-spice and ground coriander, stirring, until fragrant. Stir in sugar and juice; remove from heat. When cool enough to handle, use fingers to rub half the spice mixture into both sides of salmon fillets.

4  Place one salmon fillet on bottom half of one spring roll wrapper; top with a quarter of the leek mixture. Lightly brush edges of wrapper with blended cornflour and water; roll to enclose salmon, folding in ends. Repeat process to make a total of four salmon parcels.

5  Heat oil in large frying pan; cook parcels, in batches, until browned lightly. Place on oiled oven tray; bake parcels in oven about 8 minutes or until fish is cooked as desired.

6  Meanwhile, blend or process half the mango and remaining spice mixture until smooth. Combine remaining mango, remaining capsicum and lettuce in large bowl. Serve salmon parcels, topped with mango sauce, and salad.

**preparation time** 30 minutes
**cooking time** 15 minutes
**serves** 4
**per serving**  35.4g fat; 2677kJ (639 cal)

# prawn fritters with avocado salsa

450g cooked large prawns
2 tablespoons olive oil
1 medium brown onion (150g),
    chopped coarsely
1 clove garlic, crushed
2 teaspoons hot paprika
½ teaspoon ground cumin
¼ teaspoon ground
    white pepper
¼ teaspoon cayenne pepper
1½ cups (225g)
    self-raising flour
2 eggs
1½ cups (375ml) milk
1 tablespoon coarsely
    chopped fresh chives
2 medium avocados (500g),
    chopped coarsely
2 medium tomatoes (380g),
    chopped coarsely
1 spring onion (25g),
    trimmed, sliced thinly
2 tablespoons lime juice

1  Shell and devein prawns; chop prawn flesh coarsely.
2  Heat half the oil in large frying pan; cook brown onion, garlic and spices, stirring, until onion softens.
3  Place flour in large bowl; stir in combined eggs and milk, stirring until smooth. Stir in chives, onion mixture and prawn.
4  Heat remaining oil in same cleaned frying pan; cook ¼-cups of prawn mixture, in batches, until browned both sides.
5  Meanwhile, make avocado salsa by combing remaining ingredients in medium bowl. Serve fritters with salsa.

**preparation time** 20 minutes
**cooking time** 10 minutes
**serves** 4
**per serving**  36.7g fat; 2625kJ (627 cal)
**tips**  Fritter batter can be prepared 4 hours ahead; cover, refrigerate.
You can buy 200g of shelled prawns, if you prefer, for this recipe.

# spicy crab and prawn fritters

650g uncooked large prawns
2 x 170g cans crab meat, drained
1 tablespoon red curry paste
1 egg
2 green onions, chopped coarsely
2 tablespoons coarsely chopped fresh coriander
2 teaspoons coarsely chopped fresh lemon grass
1 fresh small red thai chilli, chopped coarsely
2 tablespoons peanut oil
chilli lime dipping sauce
2 tablespoons lime juice
2 tablespoons water
2 teaspoons fish sauce
2 teaspoons white sugar
1 kaffir lime leaf, shredded finely
1 fresh small red thai chilli, chopped finely

1  Make chilli lime dipping sauce.
2  Shell and devein prawns; blend or process prawns with crab, paste, egg, onion, coriander, lemon grass and chilli until just combined. Shape level tablespoons of mixture into fritters.
3  Heat oil in large frying pan; cook fritters, in batches, until golden brown and cooked through, drain on absorbent paper. Serve fritters with chilli lime dipping sauce.
chilli lime dipping sauce  Place ingredients in small bowl; whisk until sugar dissolves.

preparation time 20 minutes
cooking time 10 minutes
makes 30
per fritter 1.7g fat; 131kJ (31 cal)
tips To save time, buy 400g of shelled uncooked prawns.
If you can't find a kaffir lime leaf, use 1 teaspoon of finely grated lime rind.

# thai fish cakes with noodle salad

600g firm white fish fillets, chopped coarsely
1 clove garlic, crushed
1 egg white
⅔ cup loosely packed fresh coriander leaves
½ cup loosely packed fresh mint leaves
4 fresh small red thai chillies, quartered
250g rice vermicelli
2 teaspoons white sugar
¼ cup (60ml) lime juice
1 tablespoon sambal oelek
1 lebanese cucumber (130g), seeded, chopped finely
100g snow peas, sliced thinly

**1** Blend or process fish, garlic, egg white, half the coriander, half the mint and half the chilli until mixture forms a paste; shape mixture into 12 patties.
**2** Cook patties, in batches, in heated oiled large frying pan until browned both sides and cooked through.
**3** Place noodles in large heatproof bowl, cover with boiling water; stand noodles until just tender, drain. Cover to keep warm.
**4** Meanwhile, combine sugar, juice and sambal oelek in small saucepan; bring to a boil.
**5** Chop remaining coriander, mint and chilli finely. Place in large bowl with noodles, sambal mixture, cucumber and snow peas; toss to combine. Serve fish cakes on noodle salad.

**preparation time** 10 minutes
**cooking time** 20 minutes
**serves** 4
**per serving** 5.1g fat; 1566kJ (374 cal)
**tip** Redfish, usually sold skinned as fillets, is ideal for these fish cakes because of its delicate flavour. You can, however, use practically any mild-flavoured, skinless fish fillet.

# red curry fish cakes

1kg small white fish fillets, chopped coarsely
1 egg
2 teaspoons coarsely chopped fresh coriander
3 teaspoons white sugar
⅓ cup (100g) red curry paste
100g green beans, sliced thinly
vegetable oil, for deep frying

1   Blend or process fish, egg, coriander, sugar and paste until smooth.
2   Combine fish mixture and beans in large bowl; mix well.
3   Roll 2 level tablespoons of mixture into a ball, flatten slightly; repeat with remaining mixture.
4   Heat oil in large frying pan. Deep-fry fish cakes, in batches, until well browned and cooked through; drain on absorbent paper. Serve with sweet chilli sauce, if you like.

**preparation time** 10 minutes
**cooking time** 15 minutes
**makes** 25
**per fish cake** 7g fat; 424kJ (101 cal)
**tips** Fish cakes can be made a day ahead and refrigerated, covered, or frozen for up to a month.
Red curry paste is available from Asian grocery stores and most supermarkets.
We used redfish fillets for this recipe.

# fish croquettes

1 medium potato (200g)
105g can salmon, drained
1 egg, beaten lightly
2 tablespoons finely grated carrot
2 tablespoons finely grated zucchini
2 tablespoons finely grated cheddar cheese
2 tablespoons plain flour
2 teaspoons olive oil

**1** Boil, steam or microwave potato until tender; drain. Mash in small bowl; cool.
**2** Meanwhile, remove and discard bones from salmon; combine salmon, egg, carrot, zucchini and cheese with potato.
**3** Using rounded tablespoons of mixture, shape into croquettes. Toss in flour, shake away excess.
**4** Heat oil in small frying pan; cook croquettes, in batches, until browned all over. Drain on absorbent paper; serve with lemon and tomato wedges and crustless bread, if you like.

**preparation time** 20 minutes (plus cooling time)
**cooking time** 10 minutes
**serves** 2
**per serving** 14.9g fat; 1279kJ (306 cal)
**tip** You can substitute canned tuna or steamed flaked fish fillet for the salmon. Remove bones from fish before cooking.

# chicken and ham patties

1kg chicken mince
250g sliced ham, chopped finely
2 tablespoons finely chopped fresh coriander
1 clove garlic, crushed
3 green onions, chopped finely
1 cup (70g) stale breadcrumbs
¼ cup (60ml) olive oil
chilli soy dipping sauce
1 tablespoon sweet chilli sauce
2 tablespoons salt-reduced soy sauce

1   Combine all ingredients, except the oil, in large bowl. Shape
¼-cups of mixture into flat patties.
2   Heat oil in medium frying pan; cook patties, in batches, until
browned on both sides and cooked through.
3   Meanwhile, make chilli soy dipping sauce.
4   Serve patties with dipping sauce and rocket leaves, if desired.
chilli soy dipping sauce   Combine sauces in small bowl.

**preparation time** 15 minutes
**cooking time** 10 minutes
**serves** 6
**per serving** 25.3g fat; 1789kJ (427 cal)
**tip** Patties can be prepared several hours ahead.

# mini thai chicken patties with sweet chilli sauce

500g chicken thigh fillets,
   chopped coarsely
1 medium red capsicum (200g),
   chopped coarsely
2 cloves garlic, quartered
½ cup firmly packed fresh
   coriander leaves
2 fresh small red thai chillies,
   chopped coarsely
1 tablespoon fish sauce
1 egg
1½ cups (105g) stale
   breadcrumbs
2 teaspoons grated lime rind
3 green onions, chopped
   finely
vegetable oil, for deep-frying
sweet chilli sauce
½ cup (125ml) sweet chilli sauce
¼ cup (60ml) lime juice
1 clove garlic, crushed
1 tablespoon fish sauce
2 fresh small red thai chillies,
   chopped finely

1   Blend or process chicken, capsicum, garlic, coriander, chilli, sauce, egg, breadcrumbs and rind until combined.

2   Combine chicken mixture with green onion in a medium bowl. Shape tablespoonfuls of chicken mixture into patties.

3   Deep-fry patties, in batches, in hot oil until browned and cooked through; drain on absorbent paper.

4   Meanwhile, make sweet chilli sauce; serve with patties.

sweet chilli sauce  Combine ingredients in small bowl.

preparation time 15 minutes
cooking time 25 minutes
makes 35
per patty 4.1g fat; 264kJ (63 cal)

# potato pizzettas

2 chicken breast fillets (400g)
1.2kg potatoes
80g butter, melted
⅓ cup (80g) bottled pesto
6 button mushrooms (60g), sliced thinly
1 cup (100g) grated mozzarella cheese
½ cup (40g) grated parmesan cheese
¼ cup small fresh basil leaves

1  Cook chicken in heated oiled medium frying pan until cooked; stand 5 minutes then slice thinly.

2  Preheat oven to 220°C/200°C fan-forced.

3  Peel potatoes; grate coarsely into medium bowl. Cover potato with cold water; stand 5 minutes. Drain potato well; squeeze to remove excess moisture. Place potato on clean tea towel; pat dry. Combine potato and butter in cleaned medium bowl; mix well.

4  Using 6.5cm round cutter as a guide, firmly press 1 level tablespoon of the potato mixture into cutter on baking-paper-lined oven tray. Repeat with remaining mixture, allowing about 2cm between discs.

5  Bake 20 minutes. Turn; bake a further 5 minutes or until discs are browned lightly.

6  Spread potato discs with pesto; top with chicken and mushroom, sprinkle with combined cheeses. Bake about 5 minutes or until cheese melts. Top with basil leaves to serve.

**preparation time** 15 minutes
**cooking time** 40 minutes
**makes** 24
**per pizzetta** 6.9g fat; 488kJ (116 cal)
**tips** Bases can be made three hours ahead. Topping is best added just before serving.

# beef patties with tomato sauce

750g minced beef
1 cup (70g) stale breadcrumbs
⅓ cup (25g) grated parmesan cheese
1 clove garlic, crushed
2 tablespoons finely chopped fresh flat-leaf parsley
2 tablespoons finely chopped fresh basil
1 egg, beaten lightly
tomato sauce
1½ cups (375ml) bottled pasta sauce
1 small red capsicum (150g), sliced thinly
1 tablespoon coarsely chopped fresh basil

1  Make tomato sauce.
2  Combine beef, breadcrumbs, cheese, garlic, herbs and egg in large bowl; shape mixture into 12 rissoles.
3  Heat large oiled frying pan; cook rissoles until browned both sides and cooked through. Serve with tomato sauce; accompany with kumara mash, if desired.
**tomato sauce**  Combine ingredients in medium saucepan; stir over heat until sauce boils.

**preparation time** 15 minutes
**cooking time** 20 minutes
**serves** 4
**per serving**  22.1g fat; 1941kJ (463 cal)

# curry puffs with cucumber mint raita

1 tablespoon vegetable oil
2 cloves garlic, crushed
1 medium brown onion (150g),
    chopped finely
2 fresh small red thai chillies,
    chopped finely
½ teaspoon ground turmeric
2 teaspoons ground cumin
200g pork mince
1 medium potato (200g),
    chopped finely
¼ cup (30g) frozen peas
6 sheets frozen ready-rolled
    puff pastry
vegetable oil, extra,
    for deep-frying
cucumber mint raita
1 cup (280g) thick yogurt
1 lebanese cucumber (130g),
    seeded, chopped finely
2 tablespoons coarsely
    chopped fresh mint
½ teaspoon ground cumin
1 tablespoon lime juice

1   Make cucumber raita.
2   Heat oil in large frying pan; add garlic, onion, chilli, turmeric and cumin. Cook, stirring, until onion is soft. Add pork and potato; cook, stirring, until pork is well browned and potato is cooked through. Add peas; remove from heat, cool.
3   Using 8cm cutter, cut pastry into 36 rounds. Place 2 teaspoons of mixture in centre of each round. Fold rounds in half, twisting edges together to seal. Repeat with remaining pastry and pork mixture to make a total of 36 puffs.
4   Heat oil in deep large frying pan; deep-fry puffs, in batches, until golden brown. Drain on absorbent paper.
5   Serve hot puffs with cucumber mint raita.
**cucumber mint raita**  Combine ingredients in small bowl; refrigerate until required.

**preparation time** 50 minutes
(plus cooling time)
**cooking time** 10 minutes
**makes** 36
**per curry puff**  10.2g fat; 637kJ (152 cal)
**tips**  Filling can be made a day ahead; puffs can be prepared several hours ahead. Puffs are best cooked just before serving.

# little fried cheese pastries

1½ cups (225g) plain flour
½ cup (75g) self-raising flour
1 tablespoon olive oil
¾ cup (180ml) beef stock
¼ cup (50g) ricotta cheese
⅓ cup (40g) grated smoked
   cheddar cheese
½ cup (50g) grated
   mozzarella cheese
⅓ cup (25g) grated
   parmesan cheese
50g thinly sliced salami,
   chopped finely
1 egg white, beaten lightly
1 tablespoon finely chopped
   fresh rosemary
pinch ground nutmeg
vegetable oil for deep-frying

1　Sift flours into large bowl; make well in centre. Pour in small amount of combined olive oil and stock. Using one hand, work in flour a little at a time. Gradually add stock mixture, working in flour until mixture comes together in a ball.

2　Press mixture together to give a firm dough. Knead dough on lightly floured surface about 5 minutes or until dough is smooth and elastic. Cover dough with slightly damp cloth; stand 5 minutes.

3　Meanwhile, combine cheeses, salami, egg white, rosemary and nutmeg in medium bowl; mix well.

4　Roll dough on lightly floured surface until as thin as possible. Cut into 5cm rounds. Cover with slightly damp cloth to prevent dough drying out.

5　Place 1 level teaspoon of the cheese mixture in centre of each round. Brush edges of rounds with a little water. Place another round on top of cheese mixture; press edges together firmly.

6　Heat vegetable oil in large saucepan; deep-fry pastries, in batches, until browned. Drain on absorbent paper.

**preparation time** 30 minutes
**cooking time** 35 minutes
**makes** 45
**per pastry** 2.6g fat; 209kJ (50 cal)

# suppli al telefono

*This delicious snack from Italy originally got its name from the melted mozzarella "strings" that resemble telephone wires when one of these croquettes is split open and pulled apart.*

1 tablespoon olive oil
⅓ cup (40g) frozen peas
2 cloves garlic, crushed
1 cup cooked medium-grain white rice
⅓ cup (25g) finely grated parmesan cheese
1 egg, beaten lightly
1 tablespoon coarsely chopped fresh oregano
40g mozzarella cheese
½ cup (35g) stale breadcrumbs
vegetable oil, for deep-frying

**1**  Heat olive oil in large frying pan; cook peas and garlic until peas are just tender and garlic is fragrant.
**2**  Combine pea mixture in medium bowl with rice, parmesan, egg and oregano. Shape rice mixture into eight balls.
**3**  Cut mozzarella into eight cubes. Press a hole into the middle of each ball; insert one piece of the mozzarella, then re-mould rice to cover hole. Roll balls in breadcrumbs to coat all over.
**4**  Heat vegetable oil in large saucepan; deep-fry balls, in batches, until browned lightly and heated through.

**preparation time** 15 minutes
**cooking time** 15 minutes
**makes** 8
**per ball**  9.9g fat; 621kJ (148 cal)
**tip**  You need to cook about ⅓ cup of rice for this recipe.

# leek and fetta triangles

100g butter
2 cloves garlic, crushed
2 medium leeks (700g), sliced thinly
1 tablespoon caraway seeds
150g fetta cheese, chopped coarsely
⅓ cup (40g) coarsely grated cheddar cheese
4 sheets fillo pastry
2 teaspoons sesame seeds

1  Heat half the butter in large frying pan; cook garlic and leek, stirring occasionally, until leek softens. Stir in caraway seeds; cook, stirring, 2 minutes.
2  Combine leek mixture in medium bowl with fetta and cheddar.
3  Preheat oven to 200°C/180°C fan-forced. Lightly oil oven tray.
4  Melt remaining butter in small saucepan. Brush one pastry sheet lightly with butter; fold in half lengthways. Place a quarter of the leek mixture in a corner of each strip leaving a 1cm border. Fold corner with filling over, maintaining triangular shape; continue folding to end of fillo, retaining triangular shape. Place on tray, seam-side down; repeat with remaining ingredients to make four triangles in total.
5  Brush triangles with remaining melted butter; sprinkle with sesame seeds. Bake, uncovered, in oven about 10 minutes or until browned lightly.

**preparation time** 15 minutes
**cooking time** 10 minutes
**serves** 4
**per serving**  34.4g fat; 1711kJ (409 cal)

# empanadas

1 tablespoon vegetable oil
1 small brown onion (80g), chopped coarsely
2 small tomatoes (260g), seeded, chopped coarsely
1 small green capsicum (150g), chopped coarsely
2 tablespoons drained, thinly sliced, seeded black olives
2 tablespoons coarsely chopped fresh flat-leaf parsley
3 sheets ready-rolled puff pastry, thawed
1½ cups (185g) coarsely grated cheddar cheese

**1** Heat oil in medium frying pan; cook onion, tomato, capsicum and olives, stirring, until tomato just begins to soften. Remove from heat; stir through parsley. Allow filling to cool.
**2** Preheat oven to 200°C/180°C fan-forced.
**3** Using 11cm-round cutter, cut four rounds from each pastry sheet. Divide tomato filling among pastry rounds; top with equal amounts of cheese. Fold over pastry to enclose filling; pinch edges together to seal. Using knife, make two 1cm cuts in each pastry top.
**4** Place empanadas on greased oven tray; bake 15 minutes or until golden. Serve with an avocado salad and sweet chilli sauce, if you like.

**preparation time** 15 minutes (plus cooling time)
**cooking time** 20 minutes
**makes** 12
**per empanada** 16.3g fat; 934kJ (223 cal)
**tip** Filling can be prepared in advance and refrigerated, covered, until just before baking.

# corn and zucchini fritters with salsa

50g butter, melted
½ cup (125ml) milk
¾ cup (110g) plain flour
2 eggs, beaten lightly
210g can creamed corn
2 medium zucchini (240g), grated coarsely
vegetable oil, for shallow-frying
salsa
3 medium egg tomatoes (225g), chopped coarsely
2 medium avocados (500g), chopped coarsely
1 small red onion (100g), chopped coarsely
2 tablespoons lime juice
2 tablespoons finely chopped fresh coriander

1  Make salsa.
2  Combine butter, milk, flour and egg in medium bowl; whisk until smooth. Add corn and zucchini; mix well.
3  Heat oil in medium frying pan; cook heaped tablespoons of batter, one at a time, about 2 minutes each side or until browned both sides and cooked through. Drain on absorbent paper. Serve with salsa.
**salsa**  Combine ingredients in small bowl.

**preparation time** 10 minutes
**cooking time** 10 minutes
**serves** 4
**per serving** 57.6g fat; 2922kJ (698 cal)

# corn and pea samosas

1½ cups (225g) plain flour
30g ghee
1 tablespoon cumin seeds
½ cup (125ml) warm water,
    approximately
vegetable oil, for deep-frying
corn and pea filling
10g ghee
½ small brown onion (40g),
    chopped finely
1 clove garlic, crushed
1cm piece fresh ginger
    (5g), grated
1 teaspoon cumin seeds
1 teaspoon coriander seeds
2 teaspoons garam masala
¼ teaspoon ground turmeric
¼ teaspoon chilli powder
⅔ cup (110g) rinsed, drained
    canned corn kernels
⅔ cup (130g) frozen peas,
    thawed
¼ cup (60ml) coconut cream

1   Place flour in medium bowl; rub in ghee. Add seeds; gradually stir in enough of the water to mix to a firm dough. Knead on lightly floured surface about 5 minutes or until smooth. Cover; refrigerate 30 minutes.
2   Meanwhile, make corn and pea filling.
3   Roll pastry on lightly floured surface until 2mm thick. Cut pastry into 8cm rounds. Place level teaspoons of the filling into centre of each round; brush edges of pastry with water. Press edges together using thumb and finger; repeat with remaining pastry and filling to make a total of 30 samosas.
4   Heat oil in medium frying pan; deep-fry samosas, in batches, until browned lightly and cooked through.

corn and pea filling   Heat ghee in medium saucepan; add onion, garlic, ginger, seeds and spices. Cook, stirring, over low heat, until onion is soft. Add corn, peas and coconut cream; bring to a boil. Remove from heat; cool to room temperature.

preparation time 45 minutes
(plus refrigeration and cooling time)
cooking time 20 minutes
makes 30
per samosa  3.3g fat; 263kJ (63 cal)
tip  Recipe can be frozen up to four months.

# zucchini and peanut burgers

2 zucchini (200g), grated coarsely
½ cup (75g) roasted peanuts, chopped finely
2 eggs, beaten lightly
2 tablespoons finely chopped fresh flat-leaf parsley
½ cup (100g) cooked brown rice
½ cup (50g) stale breadcrumbs
⅓ cup (50g) plain flour
2 tablespoons vegetable oil
okra and tomato stew
1 tablespoon vegetable oil
1 medium brown onion (150g), sliced thinly
1 clove garlic, crushed
425g can crushed tomatoes
12 okra (150g)
1 tablespoon finely chopped fresh flat-leaf parsley

1  Make okra and tomato stew.
2  Meanwhile, squeeze excess moisture from zucchini. Combine zucchini, nuts, egg, parsley, rice and breadcrumbs in large bowl.
3  Shape mixture into six burgers; toss in flour. Heat oil in large frying pan; cook burgers until browned.
4  Serve burgers with okra and tomato stew.
**okra and tomato stew**  Heat oil in medium saucepan; cook onion and garlic, stirring, until onion is soft. Add undrained crushed tomatoes, okra and parsley; simmer, covered, 20 minutes.

**preparation time** 10 minutes
**cooking time** 30 minutes
**serves** 6
**per serving**  17.9g fat; 1301kJ (311 cal)
**tips**  Burgers can be prepared three hours ahead; refrigerate, covered.
Okra and tomato stew can be made one day ahead; refrigerate, covered.

# sesame zucchini fritters

4 medium zucchini (480g), grated coarsely
1 large potato (300g), grated coarsely
⅓ cup (50g) plain flour
1 tablespoon sesame oil
2 tablespoons sesame seeds
vegetable oil, for shallow-frying

**1** Squeeze as much liquid as possible from combined zucchini and potato; pat dry with absorbent paper.
**2** Combine vegetable mixture, flour, sesame oil and seeds in large bowl. Shape ¼-cup measures of mixture into patties.
**3** Heat vegetable oil in large frying pan; shallow fry fritters until golden brown and crisp both sides, pressing each with an egg slide to flatten well. Drain on absorbent paper; serve immediately with sea salt and freshly ground black pepper, if desired.

**preparation time** 15 minutes
**cooking time** 15 minutes
**makes** 12
**per fritter** 9.7g fat; 510kJ (122 cal)

# fennel fritters

1 tablespoon finely chopped fresh fennel fronds
1 medium fennel bulb (500g), chopped finely
3 green onions, chopped finely
1 small carrot (70g), grated finely
2 eggs, beaten lightly
75g ricotta cheese
¼ cup (35g) plain flour
2 teaspoons baking powder
vegetable oil, for shallow-frying

1  Combine fronds, fennel, onion, carrot, egg, cheese, flour and baking
powder in medium bowl; mix well.
2  Heat oil in large frying pan; shallow-fry heaped tablespoons of mixture
until golden brown both sides and cooked through. Flatten slightly during
cooking; drain on absorbent paper. Serve with mixed greens, if you like.

**preparation time** 15 minutes
**cooking time** 25 minutes
**makes** 16
**per fritter**  5.7g fat; 291kJ (70 cal)

# chive potato patties

2 large old potatoes (600g), peeled, grated coarsely
¼ cup finely chopped fresh chives
½ cup (125ml) sour cream
2 tablespoons olive oil

1  Preheat oven to 180°C/160°C fan-forced.
2  Squeeze as much liquid as possible from potato. Combine potato, chives and sour cream in large bowl; mix well. Divide mixture into eight portions; shape into 8cm patties.
3  Heat oil in large frying pan; cook patties, in batches, until browned both sides. Place patties, in single layer, on oven tray; bake, uncovered, in oven about 20 minutes or until cooked through.

**preparation time** 25 minutes
**cooking time** 30 minutes
**makes** 8
**per serving** 15.2g fat; 779kJ (186 cal)

# carrot and dill rösti

½ cup (125ml) light sour cream
1 teaspoon ground cumin
1 tablespoon finely chopped fresh dill
5 medium carrots (600g), grated
2 eggs, beaten lightly
⅓ cup (50g) plain flour

1  Combine sour cream, cumin and dill in small bowl.
2  Combine carrot, egg and flour in large bowl. Cook ¼-cup measures of carrot mixture, in batches, in heated oiled large frying pan, until browned both sides and cooked through. Serve with sour cream mixture.

**preparation time** 25 minutes
**cooking time** 35 minutes
**makes** 8
**per serving**  4.7g fat; 384kJ (92 cal)

# lentil patties with yogurt mint sauce

½ cup (100g) red lentils
½ trimmed celery stalk (50g),
    chopped finely
1 small carrot (70g),
    chopped finely
2 cups (500ml) water
½ teaspoon ground coriander
½ teaspoon ground cumin
2 cups (140g) stale
    breadcrumbs
2 tablespoons plain flour
1 egg white, beaten lightly
1 tablespoon finely chopped
    fresh flat-leaf parsley
1 tablespoon olive oil
yogurt mint sauce
½ cup (125ml) low-fat yogurt
1 tablespoon finely chopped
    fresh mint
1 clove garlic, crushed
1 teaspoon lemon juice

1   Combine lentils, celery, carrot, the water, coriander and cumin in large saucepan; bring to a boil. Reduce heat; simmer, covered, about 20 minutes or until mixture thickens; cool.
2   Stir in half the breadcrumbs. Shape lentil mixture into four patties; toss in flour. Dip in egg white; dip in combined remaining breadcrumbs and parsley.
3   Heat oil in large frying pan; cook patties until well browned both sides. Drain on absorbent paper.
4   Meanwhile, make yogurt mint sauce.
5   Serve patties with yogurt mint sauce and a green leaf salad, if desired.
**yogurt mint sauce**   Combine ingredients in small bowl; mix well.

**preparation time** 20 minutes
(plus cooling time)
**cooking time** 30 minutes
**serves** 2
**per serving** 14.3g fat; 2433kJ (582 cal)
**tips** Uncooked patties and yogurt mint sauce can be made one day ahead and refrigerated, covered, separately. Uncooked patties can be frozen up to six months.

# lentil balls with tomatoes and rocket

1 cup (200g) red lentils
2 tablespoons olive oil
2 medium zucchini (240g),
    grated coarsely
1 small brown onion (80g),
    chopped finely
1 fresh small red thai chilli,
    chopped finely
1 cup (70g) stale breadcrumbs
¼ cup (35g) white sesame
    seeds, toasted
1 tablespoon finely chopped
    fresh coriander
⅓ cup (35g) packaged
    breadcrumbs
vegetable oil for deep-frying
5 medium egg tomatoes
    (375g), quartered
2 cloves garlic, crushed
120g rocket
2 tablespoons shredded
    fresh mint
2 tablespoons shredded
    fresh basil
¼ cup (60ml) white wine
    vinegar

1  Add lentils to large saucepan of boiling water; boil, uncovered, about 8 minutes or until just tender. Drain; press out liquid.

2  Meanwhile, heat half the olive oil in large frying pan; stir-fry zucchini, onion and chilli until onion is just soft.

3  Combine lentils, zucchini mixture, stale breadcrumbs, seeds and coriander in medium bowl. Roll teaspoonfuls of the mixture into balls; toss in packaged breadcrumbs.

4  Heat vegetable oil in large frying pan. Deep-fry balls, in batches, until browned; drain on absorbent paper.

5  Heat remaining olive oil in same frying pan; stir-fry tomato and garlic 2 minutes. Return lentil balls to pan; stir until heated through.

6  Remove pan from heat. Add remaining ingredients; toss to combine.

**preparation time** 30 minutes
**cooking time** 25 minutes
**serves** 4
**per serving**  16.5g fat; 1924kJ (460 cal)

# soya patties with lemon and herb yogurt

1 tablespoon olive oil

1 medium red onion (170g),
chopped finely

1 medium red capsicum
(200g), chopped finely

2 cloves garlic, crushed

3 cups (210g) stale
breadcrumbs

2 x 300g cans soy beans,
rinsed, drained

2 eggs, beaten lightly

½ cup finely chopped fresh
flat-leaf parsley

2 teaspoons grated lemon rind

¾ cup (60g) grated parmesan
cheese

⅓ cup (50g) roasted pine nuts

lemon and herb yogurt

200g yogurt

1 clove garlic, crushed

1 tablespoon lemon juice

2 tablespoons finely chopped
fresh flat-leaf parsley

2 tablespoons finely chopped
fresh chives

1 Preheat oven to 220°C/200°C fan-forced.

2 Heat oil in medium saucepan; cook onion,
capsicum and garlic, stirring, until onion is soft.

3 Process breadcrumbs, beans, egg, parsley,
rind, half the cheese and onion mixture until
just combined; stir in nuts.

4 Shape ⅓-cup measures of the mixture
into patties. Place patties on oiled baking
tray; sprinkle with remaining cheese. Bake in
oven about 20 minutes or until browned lightly,
turning halfway through cooking.

5 Meanwhile, make lemon and herb yogurt.

6 Serve patties with lemon and herb yogurt and
steamed asparagus and rocket leaves, if desired.

lemon and herb yogurt Combine ingredients
in small bowl.

preparation time 20 minutes
cooking time 25 minutes
serves 4
per serving 30g fat; 2416kJ (577 cal)
tips Recipe can be made one day ahead
and refrigerated, covered. Uncooked patties
can be frozen up to four months.

# gorgonzola fritters

1 cup (200g) ricotta cheese
1 cup (185g) coarsely chopped gorgonzola cheese
2 eggs, beaten lightly
½ cup (75g) plain flour
vegetable oil for deep-frying
1 cup (80g) finely grated parmesan cheese

1   Combine ricotta, gorgonzola and egg in medium bowl. Whisk
in flour; stand at room temperature for 1 hour.
2   Heat oil in large saucepan; deep-fry heaped teaspoons of
mixture, turning occasionally, until fritters are browned lightly all
over and cooked through. (Do not have oil too hot or fritters will
over-brown before cooking through).
3   Place parmesan in medium bowl; toss fritters, in batches, to
coat as they are cooked. Sprinkle fritters with extra grated parmesan
before serving, if desired.

**preparation time** 15 minutes (plus standing time)
**cooking time** 5 minutes
**makes** 36
**per serving**  4g fat; 231kJ (55 cal)
**tip**  Gorgonzola is a creamy blue cheese from Italy; if unavailable
use blue castello or a similar soft blue cheese.

# glossary

**basil** we use sweet, or common, basil unless otherwise stated.

**buk choy** also known as bak choy, pak choi, chinese white cabbage or chinese chard; has a fresh, mild mustard taste. *Baby buk choy, also known as pak kat farang, shanghai bok choy, chinese chard or white cabbage, is smaller and more tender than buk choy.*

**butter** use salted or unsalted (sweet) butter; 125g is equal to one stick of butter.

**capsicum** also known as pepper or bell pepper.

**cayenne pepper** extremely hot, dried red chilli, usually purchased ground.

**cheese**
**cheddar** a semi-hard cow-milk cheese. It ranges in colour from white to pale yellow, and has a slightly crumbly texture.
**cheddar, smoked** a hard cheddar cheese that has been placed, uncut, in a smoke room for about six hours. Artificially smoked cheese, where flavour is added before the cheese is made, is also available.
**fetta** salty white cheese with milky, fresh acidity. Can be made from either cow, sheep or goats' milk.
**gorgonzola** a creamy blue cheese (mould-treated and mottled with blue veining) having a mild, sweet taste.

**mozzarella** a soft, spun-curd cheese; it has a low melting point and elastic texture when heated, and is used to add texture rather than flavour.
**parmesan** also known as parmigiano; a hard, grainy cow-milk cheese.
**ricotta** a sweet, moist cheese; the name for this soft, white, cow-milk cheese roughly translates as "cooked again". It's made from whey, a by-product of other cheese-making, to which fresh milk and acid are added.

**chilli**
**powder** the Asian variety, made from dried ground thai chillies, is the hottest; it can be used as a substitute for fresh chillies in the proportion of ½ teaspoon ground chilli powder to 1 medium chopped fresh chilli.
**red thai** also known as "scuds"; tiny, very hot and bright red in colour.

**coconut**
**cream** commercially obtained from the first pressing of the coconut flesh, without the addition of water; the second pressing (less rich) is sold as coconut milk. Available in cans and cartons at supermarkets.
**desiccated** unsweetened, concentrated, dried, finely shredded coconut.

**coriander** also known as pak chee, cilantro or chinese parsley; bright-green leafy herb with a pungent flavour. Also sold as seeds, whole or ground.

**cornflour** also known as cornstarch. Available made from corn or wheat.

**crab meat** flesh of fresh crabs; frozen flesh is also available. Use canned if either is unavailable.

**cucumber, lebanese** short, slender and thin-skinned. Probably the most popular variety because of its tender, edible skin, tiny, yielding seeds and sweet, fresh and flavoursome taste.

**cumin** also known as zeera or comino; the dried seed of a plant related to the parsley family. Has a spicy, almost curry-like, flavour.

**curry powder** a blend of ground spices. Choose mild or hot to suit your taste.

**fennel** also known as finocchio or anise.

**fish fillets, firm white** any boneless firm white fish fillet; blue eye, bream, swordfish, ling, whiting or sea perch are all good choices. Check for small pieces of bone in the fillets and use tweezers to remove them.

**five-spice powder** a mixture of ground cloves, cinnamon, star anise, fennel seeds and sichuan pepper. Also known as chinese five-spice.

**flat-leaf parsley** also known as continental or italian parsley.

**flour**

**plain** also known as all-purpose flour.

**self-raising** all-purpose plain flour with baking powder added in the proportion of 1 cup flour to 2 teaspoons baking powder.

**garam masala** a blend of spices based on cloves, cardamom, cinnamon, coriander, fennel and cumin.

**ginger** also known as green or root ginger; the thick root of a tropical plant.

**kaffir lime leaves** also known as bai magrood; look like two glossy dark green leaves joined end to end, forming a rounded hourglass shape. A strip of fresh lime peel may be substituted for each kaffir lime leaf.

**lemon grass** also known as takrai, serai or serah. A tall, clumping, lemon-smelling and tasting, sharp-edged aromatic tropical grass; the white lower part of the stem is used, finely chopped, in cooking.

**lettuce, red coral** has very curly and tightly furled leaves that look like coral; comes in distinctive tasting red and green leaves.

**mince meat** also known as ground meat, as in beef, pork, lamb and chicken.

**okra** also known as bamia or lady fingers. A green, ridged, oblong pod with a furry skin.

**paprika** ground dried sweet red capsicum (bell pepper); many types are available, including sweet, hot, mild and smoked.

**pastry**

**fillo** also known as phyllo or filo; tissue-thin pastry sheets purchased chilled or frozen.

**ready-rolled puff** packaged sheets of frozen puff pastry, available from supermarkets.

**pesto** a paste made from fresh basil, oil, garlic, pine nuts and parmesan.

**pide** also known as turkish bread; comes in long (about 45cm) flat loaves as well as individual rounds. Made from wheat flour.

**potato, sebago** oval in shape with a white skin; good fried, mashed and baked.

**prawns** also known as shrimp. Varieties include; royal red, school, sydney harbour, king, tiger. Can be bought uncooked (green) or cooked, with or without shells.

**rice vermicelli** also known as sen mee, mei fun or bee hoon. Soak in hot water until softened, then boil briefly and rinse with hot water.

**sambal oelek** (also spelled ulek or olek) Indonesian in origin; a salty paste with medium heat, made from ground chillies and vinegar.

**sauce**

**fish** called naam pla or nuoc naam. Made from pulverised salted fermented fish (most often anchovies); has a pungent smell and strong taste, so use sparingly.

**soy** also known as sieu; made from fermented soy beans. Several variations are available in supermarkets and Asian food stores.

**sweet chilli** mild, fairly sticky bottled sauce made from red chillies, sugar, garlic and white wine vinegar; mostly used as a condiment.

**snow peas** a variety of garden pea, also called mange tout (eat all); eaten pod and all (though you may need to trim the ends).

**spring roll wrappers** also called egg roll wrappers; come in various sizes and can be purchased fresh or frozen.

**sugar**

**palm** also known as nam tan pip, jaggery, jawa or gula melaka; made from the sap of the sugar palm tree. Light brown to black in colour and usually sold in rock-hard cakes; substitute with brown sugar if unavailable.

**white** also known as crystal or granulated table sugar.

**turmeric** also known as kamin; a rhizome related to galangal and ginger.

**zucchini** also known as courgette.

# conversion chart

## MEASURES

One Australian metric measuring cup holds approximately 250ml, one Australian metric tablespoon holds 20ml, one Australian metric teaspoon holds 5ml.

The difference between one country's measuring cups and another's is within a 2- or 3-teaspoon variance, and will not affect your cooking results. North America, New Zealand and the United Kingdom use a 15ml tablespoon. All cup and spoon measurements are level. The most accurate way of measuring dry ingredients is to weigh them. When measuring liquids, use a clear glass or plastic jug with metric markings.

We use large eggs with an average weight of 60g.

## DRY MEASURES

| METRIC | IMPERIAL |
|---|---|
| 15g | ½oz |
| 30g | 1oz |
| 60g | 2oz |
| 90g | 3oz |
| 125g | 4oz (¼lb) |
| 155g | 5oz |
| 185g | 6oz |
| 220g | 7oz |
| 250g | 8oz (½lb) |
| 280g | 9oz |
| 315g | 10oz |
| 345g | 11oz |
| 375g | 12oz (¾lb) |
| 410g | 13oz |
| 440g | 14oz |
| 470g | 15oz |
| 500g | 16oz (1lb) |
| 750g | 24oz (1½lb) |
| 1kg | 32oz (2lb) |

## LIQUID MEASURES

| METRIC | IMPERIAL |
|---|---|
| 30ml | 1 fluid oz |
| 60ml | 2 fluid oz |
| 100ml | 3 fluid oz |
| 125ml | 4 fluid oz |
| 150ml | 5 fluid oz (¼ pint/1 gill) |
| 190ml | 6 fluid oz |
| 250ml | 8 fluid oz |
| 300ml | 10 fluid oz (½ pint) |
| 500ml | 16 fluid oz |
| 600ml | 20 fluid oz (1 pint) |
| 1000ml (1 litre) | 1¾ pints |

## LENGTH MEASURES

| METRIC | IMPERIAL |
|---|---|
| 3mm | ⅛in |
| 6mm | ¼in |
| 1cm | ½in |
| 2cm | ¾in |
| 2.5cm | 1in |
| 5cm | 2in |
| 6cm | 2½in |
| 8cm | 3in |
| 10cm | 4in |
| 13cm | 5in |
| 15cm | 6in |
| 18cm | 7in |
| 20cm | 8in |
| 23cm | 9in |
| 25cm | 10in |
| 28cm | 11in |
| 30cm | 12in (1ft) |

## OVEN TEMPERATURES

These oven temperatures are only a guide for conventional ovens. For fan-forced ovens, check the manufacturer's manual.

| | °C (CELSIUS) | °F (FAHRENHEIT) | GAS MARK |
|---|---|---|---|
| Very slow | 120 | 250 | ½ |
| Slow | 150 | 275 – 300 | 1 – 2 |
| Moderately slow | 160 | 325 | 3 |
| Moderate | 180 | 350 – 375 | 4 – 5 |
| Moderately hot | 200 | 400 | 6 |
| Hot | 220 | 425 – 450 | 7 – 8 |
| Very hot | 240 | 475 | 9 |

# index

# Are you missing some of the world's favourite cookbooks?

*The Australian Women's Weekly* cookbooks are available from bookshops, cookshops, supermarkets and other stores all over the world. You can also buy direct from the publisher, using the order form below.

## MINI SERIES £3.50 190x138MM 64 PAGES

| TITLE | QTY | TITLE | QTY | TITLE | QTY |
|---|---|---|---|---|---|
| 4 Fast Ingredients | | Drinks | | Pasta | |
| 15-minute Feasts | | Easy Pies & Pastries | | Potatoes | |
| 50 Fast Chicken Fillets | | Finger Food | | Roast | |
| 50 Fast Desserts | | Fishcakes & Crispybakes | | Salads | |
| 50 Fast Prawns (Oct 07) | | Gluten-free Cooking | | Simple Slices | |
| After-work Stir-fries | | Healthy Everyday Food 4 Kids | | Simply Seafood | |
| Barbecue Chicken | | Ice-creams & Sorbets | | Skinny Food | |
| Bites | | Indian Cooking | | Spanish Favourites | |
| Bowl Food | | Italian Favourites | | Stir-fries | |
| Burgers, Rösti & Fritters | | Jams & Jellies | | Summer Salads | |
| Cafe Cakes | | Japanese Favourites | | Tagines & Couscous | |
| Cafe Food | | Kebabs & Skewers | | Tapas, Antipasto & Mezze | |
| Casseroles | | Kids Party Food | | Tarts | |
| Casseroles & Curries | | Last-minute Meals | | Tex-Mex | |
| Char-grills & Barbecues | | Lebanese Cooking | | Thai Favourites | |
| Cheesecakes, Pavlova & Trifles | | Low-Fat Delicious | | The Fast Egg | |
| Chinese Favourites | | Malaysian Favourites | | Vegetarian | |
| Christmas Cakes & Puddings | | Mince | | Vegie Main Meals | |
| Christmas Favourites (Oct 07) | | Mince Favourites | | Vietnamese Favourites | |
| Cocktails | | Muffins | | Wok | |
| Crumbles & Bakes | | Noodles | | | |
| Cupcakes & Cookies | | Noodles & Stir-fries | | | |
| Curries | | Outdoor Eating | | | |
| Dips & Dippers | | Party Food | | | |
| Dried Fruit & Nuts | | Pickles and Chutneys | | TOTAL COST £ | |

*Photocopy and complete coupon below*

Name _____

Address _____

_____ Postcode _____

Country _____ Phone (business hours) _____

Email*(optional) _____

*\* By including your email address, you consent to receipt of any email regarding this magazine, and other emails which inform you of ACP's other publications, products, services and events, and to promote third party goods and services you may be interested in.*

I enclose my cheque/money order for £ _____ or please charge £ _____

to my: ☐ Access ☐ Mastercard ☐ Visa ☐ Diners Club

Card number | | | | | | | | | | | | | | | |

3 digit security code *(found on reverse of card)* _____

Cardholder's
signature _____ Expiry date ____ /____

**To order:** Mail or fax – photocopy or complete the order form above, and send your credit card details or cheque payable to: Australian Consolidated Press (UK), 10 Scirocco Close, Moulton Park Office Village, Northampton NN3 6AP, phone (+44) (01) 604 642200, fax (+44) (01) 604 642300, e-mail books@acpuk.com or order online at www.acpuk.com
**Non-UK residents:** We accept the credit cards listed on the coupon, or cheques, drafts or International Money Orders payable in sterling and drawn on a UK bank. Credit card charges are at the exchange rate current at the time of payment.
All pricing current at time of going to press and subject to change/availability.
**Postage and packing UK:** Add £1.00 per order plus 75p per book.
**Postage and packing overseas:** Add £2.00 per order plus £1.50 per book. **Offer ends 31.12.2008**